롤러코스터
이래서 강력추천합니다!

체계적인 학습 │ 초등학교 교육 과정을 충실히 반영하고 교과서 지문을 최대한 활용함으로써 학생들이 배워야 할 주요 학습 내용을 체계적으로 익힐 수 있도록 하였습니다.

학년별 맞춤 학습 │ 모든 학년에서 표현과 낱말 학습을 기본으로 하되, 1·2학년은 Phonics, 3·4학년은 Reading & Writing, 5·6학년은 Grammar를 다루는 등, 각 학년별 주요 학습 영역을 중점적으로 다룸으로써 학년별 맞춤 학습을 추구하였습니다.

균형적인 학습 │ 읽기, 쓰기 학습뿐만 아니라 오디오 CD와 동영상 CD를 활용한 듣기, 말하기 학습을 통해 영어의 4개 영역(Listening, Speaking, Reading, Writing)을 고루 마스터할 수 있도록 하였습니다.

자발적인 학습 │ Song, Chant를 통해 표현을 자연스럽게 익히고, Cartoon을 통해 배운 내용을 재미있게 정리하는 등 다양한 Activity를 통해 학생들이 흥미를 가지고 적극적으로 수업에 참여할 수 있도록 하였습니다.

동영상을 통한 원어민과의 학습 │ 원어민의 발음과 입모양을 동영상 CD를 통해 정확히 인지하고 학습자의 발음을 녹음해 원어민의 발음과 비교하여 들어 보게 함으로써 학습자 스스로 발음을 교정할 수 있는 기회를 제공하였습니다.

01 Student Book

신나는 챈트를 듣고 따라 부르며,
알파벳과 낱말을 익혀 봐요.

그림 속에서 짝이 되는 대소문자를
찾아 손으로 짚어보며 익혀봐요.

각 대문자와 짝이 되는 소문자 스티커를 찾아
붙이며 그림을 완성해 봐요.

● 각 문자의 소리와 그 소리가 들어있는
　낱말을 듣고 따라 말해 봐요.

● 다양한 Activity를 통해 학습한 문자를
　확인해 봐요.

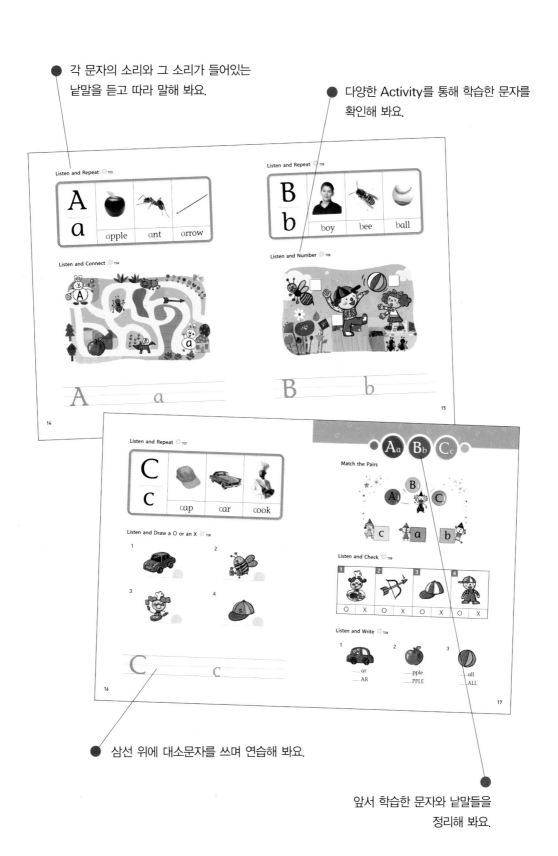

● 삼선 위에 대소문자를 쓰며 연습해 봐요.

앞서 학습한 문자와 낱말들을
정리해 봐요.

02 Workbook

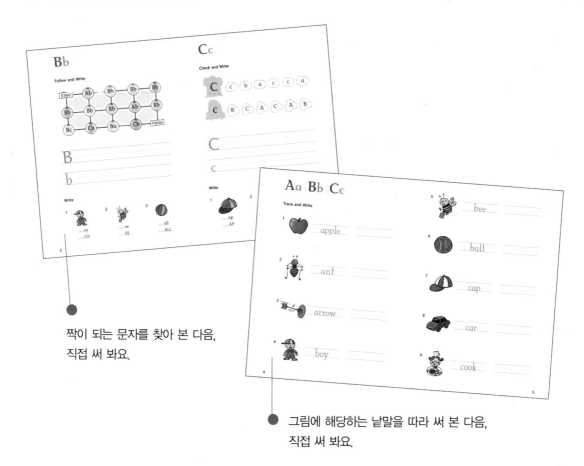

짝이 되는 문자를 찾아 본 다음,
직접 써 봐요.

그림에 해당하는 낱말을 따라 써 본 다음,
직접 써 봐요.

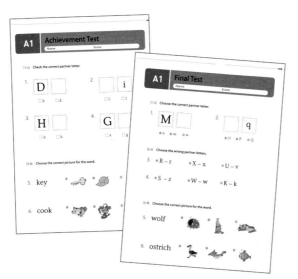

03 권말 테스트

테스트를 통해 학습한 문자 및 낱말에 대한
학습 성취도를 점검해 봐요.
(Achievement Test / Final Test)

04 동영상 CD

Learn

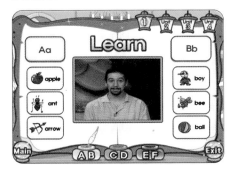

대소문자와 각 글자의 소리 및 그 소리가
들어있는 낱말을 알아봐요.

Speak

학습한 낱말들을 녹음해 원어민의 발음과
비교해 봐요.

Song

신나는 알파벳 송을 부르며 알파벳을
정리해 봐요.

Game

재미있는 게임을 하며 학습한 낱말들을
확인해 봐요.

05 오디오 CD

Student Book, Workbook의 내용과 노래 및
챈트가 담겨 있어요.

Learning Points

A1

Unit Title	Topic	Vocabulary
❶ Learning Aa~Ff	· Aa, Bb, Cc, Dd, Ee, Ff	apple, ant, arrow, boy, bee, ball, cap, car, cook, dog, dad, door, elbow, egg, elephant, flag, fish, fan
❷ Learning Gg~Ll	· Gg, Hh, Ii, Jj, Kk, Ll	girl, goat, guitar, house, hand, hat, iguana, insect, igloo, jacket, jeans, juice, kitten, king, key, leaf, lily, lion
❸ Learning Mm~Ss	· Mm, Nn, Oo, Pp, Qq, Rr, Ss	mouse, milk, moon, nest, nose, nurse, ostrich, orange, octopus, pig, piano, pear, question, queen, quilt, rabbit, robot, rose, sun, socks, shoes
❹ Learning Tt~Zz	· Tt, Uu , Vv, Ww, Xx, Yy, Zz	tiger, table, tent, up, umbrella, ugly, vest, violin, van, wolf, witch, web, fox, ox, box, yawn, yo-yo, yacht, zebra, zipper, zoo

A2

Unit Title	Function	Conversation	Phonics
① My Name Is Leo	· Greeting · Asking and giving names	Hi. My name is Meg. What's your name? My name is Leo. Bye.	First sounds P and B
② This Is a Chair	· Identifying objects in classroom	That is a desk. This is a chair.	First sounds T and D
③ What's This?	· Identifying school supplies	What's this(that)? It's a bag(book).	First sounds K and G
④ It's Pink	· Identifying colors	What color is this? It's pink. It's yellow.	First sounds F and V

A3

Unit Title	Function	Conversation	Phonics
① She Is My Mother	· Identifying family members	Who is he(she)? He(She) is my father (mother).	First sounds S and Z
② Are You Happy?	· Asking and telling about feelings	Are you happy? Yes, I am. No, I'm not.	First sounds H and J
③ It's Sunny	· Asking about and describing the weather	How's the weather? It's sunny.	First sounds M and N
④ Put On Your Gloves	· Commands	It's cold. Put on your gloves. OK, Mom.	First sounds L and R

Basic Commands

Roller Coaster
Contents

UNIT 01 Learning Aa~Ff

Ee

Ff

Dd

Stick on the Partner Letters

A B C

🎵 **Let's Chant** ⊙ T02

Aa Aa Aa Aa is for 🍎

Bb Bb Bb Bb is for 👦

Cc Cc Cc Cc is for

Dd Dd Dd Dd is for 🐕

Ee Ee Ee Ee is for

Ff Ff Ff Ff is for 🚩

Aa

Bb

Cc

D E F

Listen and Repeat T03

| A a | apple | ant | arrow |

Listen and Connect T04

A   a

Listen and Repeat  T05

| | boy | bee | ball |

Listen and Number T06

B   b

Listen and Repeat T07

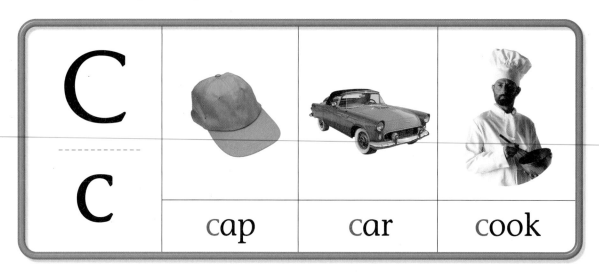

| C c | cap | car | cook |

Listen and Draw a O or an X T08

1

2

3

4

C   c

Match the Pairs

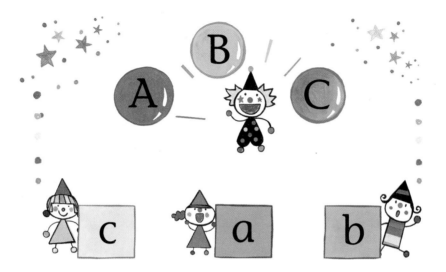

Listen and Check T09

1	2	3	4
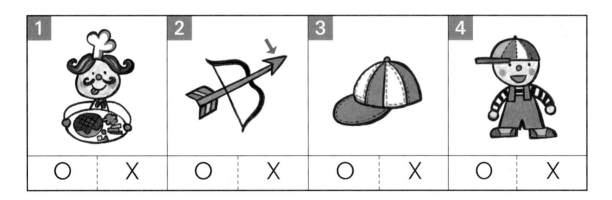			
O X	O X	O X	O X

Listen and Write T09

1

＿＿ar
＿＿AR

2

＿＿pple
＿＿PPLE

3

＿＿all
＿＿ALL

Listen and Repeat T10

| D d | dog | dad | door |

Listen and Mark T11

dad △

dog ○

door ☆

D   d

Listen and Repeat T12

| elbow | egg | elephant |

Listen and Circle ⊙ T13

1

2

3
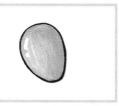  

E   e

Listen and Repeat T14

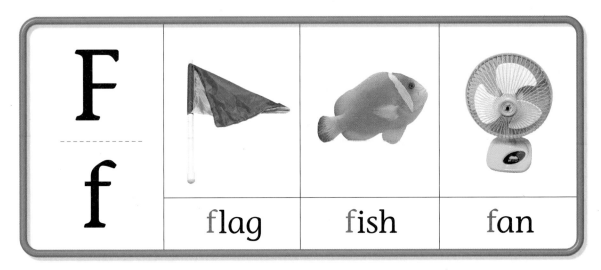

| F f | flag | fish | fan |

Listen and Number T15

F   f

Match the Pairs

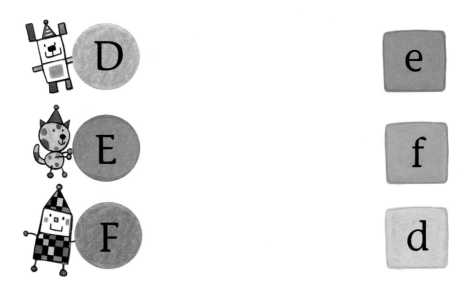

Listen and Check T16

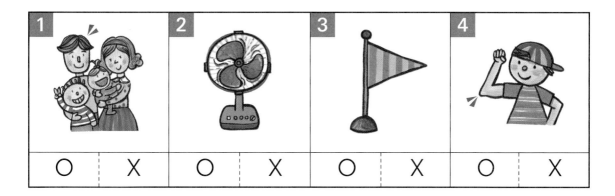

Listen and Write T16

1 ___ish
___ISH

2 ___lephant
___LEPHANT

3 ___oor
___OOR

21

Learning Gg~Ll

Hh

Gg

Ll

Stick on the Partner Letters

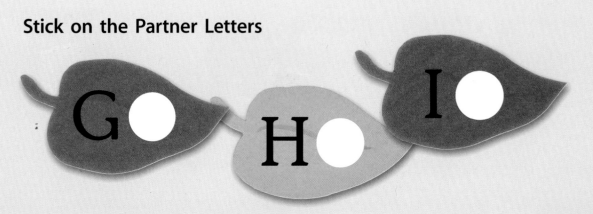

G ○

H ○

I ○

Gg Gg Gg Gg is for

Hh Hh Hh Hh is for

Ii Ii Ii Ii is for

Jj Jj Jj Jj is for

Kk Kk Kk Kk is for

Ll Ll Ll Ll is for

Ii

Jj

Kk

J K L

23

Listen and Repeat T18

| G g | girl | goat | guitar |

Listen and Circle T19

1

2

3

G   g

Listen and Repeat T20

| H h | house | hand | hat |

Listen and Mark T21

hat △

house ○

hand ☆

H   h

Listen and Repeat T22

| I i | iguana | insect | igloo |

Listen and Number T23

I i

Draw a O or an X

H h	I g	I i
I h	G g	H i

Listen and Check ⊙ T24

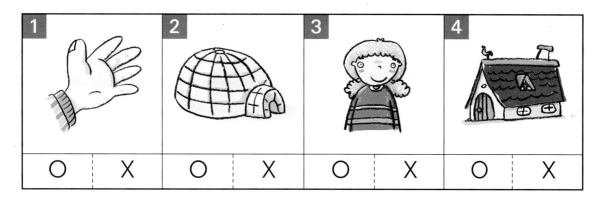

1	2	3	4
O : X	O : X	O : X	O : X

Listen and Write ⊙ T24

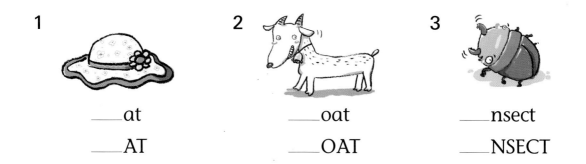

1 ___at
___AT

2 ___oat
___OAT

3 ___nsect
___NSECT

Listen and Repeat T25

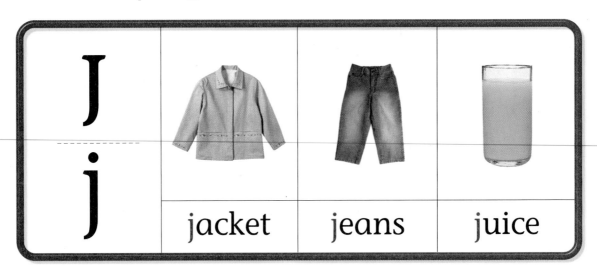

| J j | jacket | jeans | juice |

Listen and Check T26

1 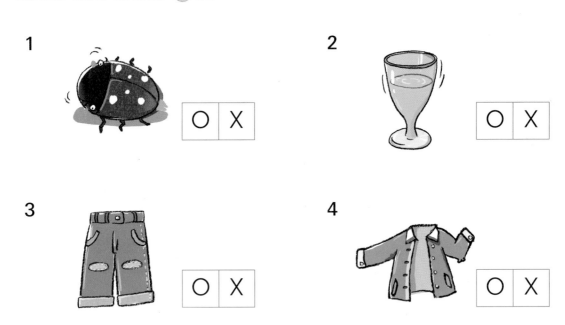 O X

2 O X

3 O X

4 O X

J   j

Listen and Repeat T27

K **k**	kitten	king	key

Listen and Connect T28

Listen and Repeat T29

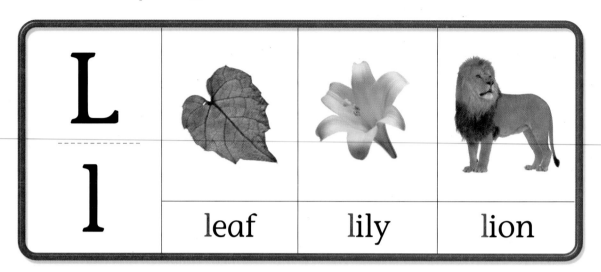

| L l | leaf | lily | lion |

Listen and Draw a O or an X T30

1

2

3

4

L   l

Match the Pairs

 ·

 ·

 ·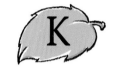

Listen and Check ◎ T31

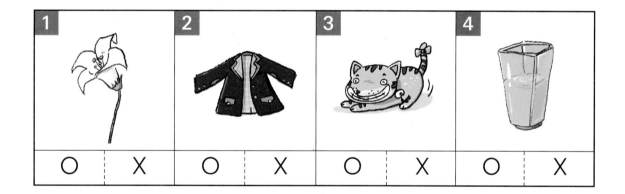

1		2		3		4	
O	X	O	X	O	X	O	X

Listen and Write ◎ T31

1
____ion
____ION

2
____ey
____EY

3
____eans
____EANS

Pp

Mm

Rr

Stick on the Partner Letters

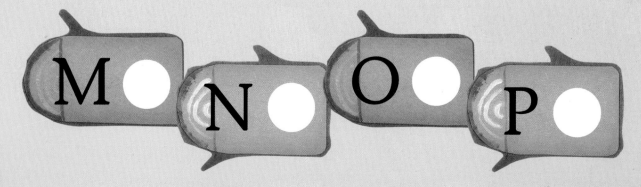

M   N   O   P

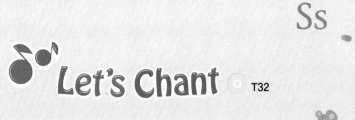

🎵 **Let's Chant** T32

Mm Mm Mm Mm is for

Nn Nn Nn Nn is for

Oo Oo Oo Oo is for

Pp Pp Pp Pp is for

Qq Qq Qq Qq is for **?**

Rr Rr Rr Rr is for

Ss Ss Ss Ss is for

Listen and Repeat T33

| M m | mouse | milk | moon |

Listen and Connect T34

M m

Listen and Repeat T35

| | nest | nose | nurse |

Listen and Draw a O or an X T36

1

2

3

4

Listen and Repeat  T37

O
o

ostrich | orange | octopus

Listen and Circle T38

1

2

3

O   o

Circle the Partner Letter

Listen and Circle T39

1 | m | / | n | ilk

2 | m | / | n | est

3 | m | / | n | urse

4 | m | / | n | oon

Listen and Write T39

1

___strich

___STRICH

2

___ose

___OSE

3

___ouse

___OUSE

Listen and Repeat T40

| P p | pig | piano | pear |

Listen and Check T41

1
 ○ X

2
 ○ X

3
 ○ X

4
 ○ X

P

p

Listen and Repeat T42

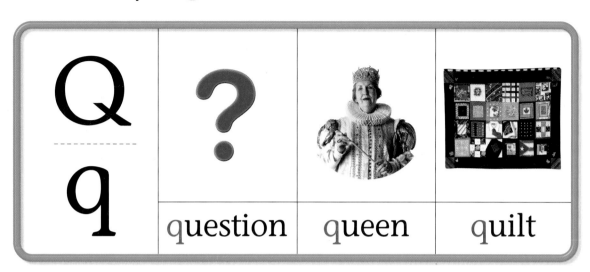

Q q	?		
	question	queen	quilt

Listen and Draw a O or an X T43

1

2

3

4

Q   q

Listen and Repeat T44

R r	rabbit	robot	rose

Listen and Mark T45

rose △

robot ○

rabbit ☆

R   r

Listen and Repeat T46

S s	sun	socks	shoes

Listen and Number T47

S   s

Match the Pairs

P R Q S

q r p s

Listen and Check T48

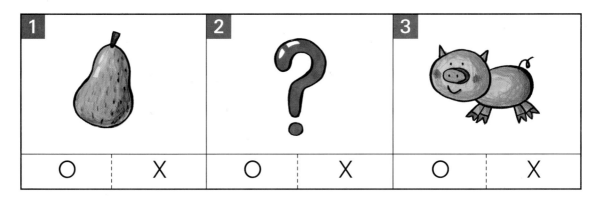

1	2	3
O · X	O · X	O · X

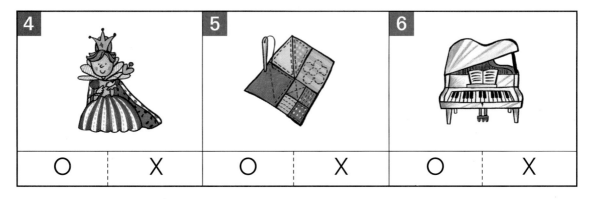

4	5	6
O · X	O · X	O · X

Listen and Circle T48

1

r
s
abbit

2

r
s
un

3

r
s
ocks

4

r
s
obot

5

r
s
ose

6

r
s
hoes

Listen and Write T48

1

___uilt

___UILT

2

___iano

___IANO

3

___obot

___OBOT

4

___ose

___OSE

5

___ear

___EAR

6

___hoes

___HOES

Learning Tt~Zz

Stick on the Partner Letters

 T  U  V

 **Let's Chant** T49

Tt Tt Tt Tt is for

Uu Uu Uu Uu is for

Vv Vv Vv Vv is for

Ww Ww Ww Ww is for

Xx Xx Xx Xx is for

Yy Yy Yy Yy is for

Zz Zz Zz Zz is for

Listen and Repeat 🔊 T50

| T t | tiger | table | tent |

Listen and Connect 🔊 T51

T   t

Listen and Repeat T52

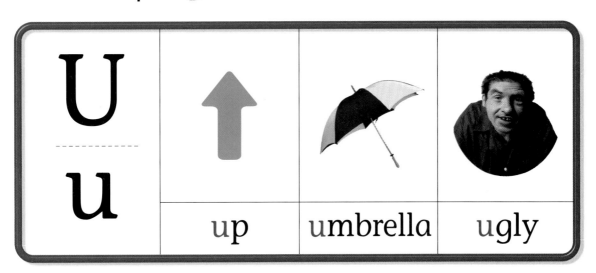

| U
u | ↑
up | umbrella | ugly |

Listen and Draw a O or an X T53

1

2

3

4

Listen and Repeat  T54

V v	vest	violin	van

Listen and Number T55

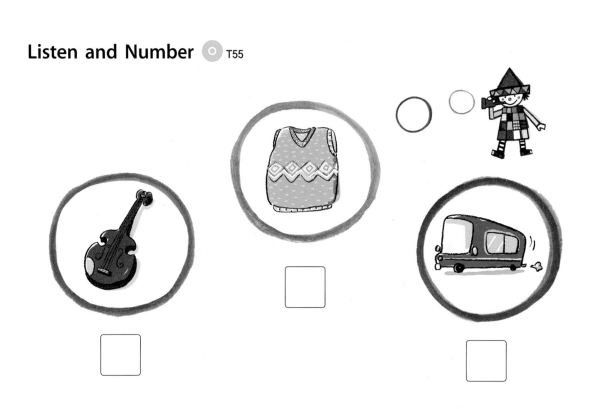

Circle the Pairs

Listen and Circle

1 
| t |
| u |
gly

2 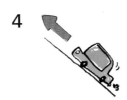
| t |
| u |
iger

3
| t |
| u |
able

4 
| t |
| u |
p

Listen and Write

1

＿iolin

＿IOLIN

2

＿ent

＿ENT

3

＿mbrella

＿MBRELLA

49

Listen and Repeat T57

W w	wolf	witch	web

Listen and Check T58

1

O X

2
O X

3
O X

4
O X

Listen and Repeat T59

| X x | fox | ox | box |

Listen and Circle T60

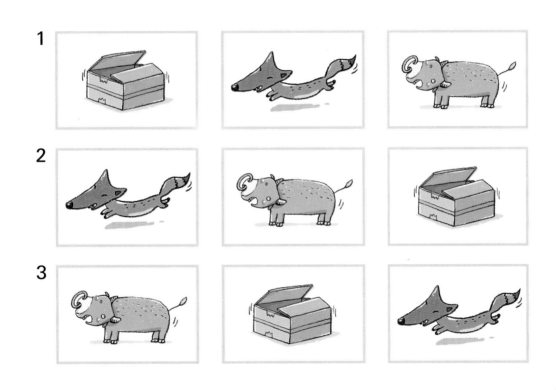

X   x

Listen and Repeat T61

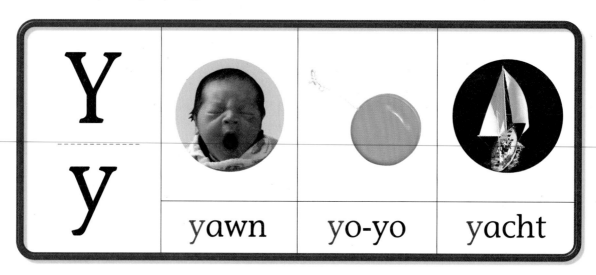

| Y y | yawn | yo-yo | yacht |

Listen and Number T62

Y   y

Listen and Repeat T63

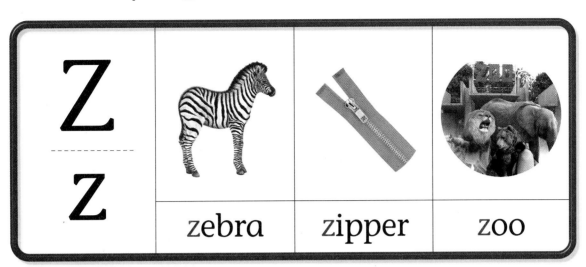

| Z z | zebra | zipper | zoo |

Listen and Draw a O or an X T64

1

2

3

4

Z   z

Match the Pairs

W   X   Y   Z

y   w   z   x

Listen and Check  T65

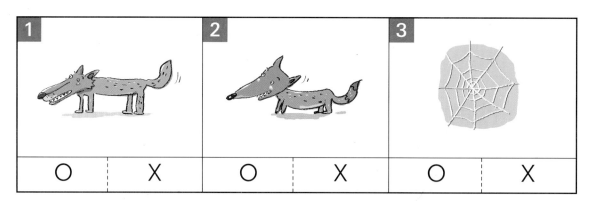

1	2	3
O X	O X	O X

4	5	6
O X	O X	O X

Listen and Circle 🔘 T65

1

y
z
o-yo

2

y
z
ebra

3

y
z
awn

4

y
z
ipper

5

y
z
oo

6

y
z
acht

Listen and Write 🔘 T65

1

___itch

___ITCH

2

___o-yo

___O-YO

3

___ipper

___IPPER

4

o___

O___

5

___awn

___AWN

6

___eb

___EB

Pick up the Eggs

준비물 : 주사위, 마커

❶ 각자 마커를 정하고 가위바위보를 한 후, 이긴 순서대로 주사위를 굴리세요.

❷ 주사위가 짝수로 나오면 한 칸, 홀수로 나오면 두 칸을 가세요.

❸ 도착한 자리의 그림을 보고 그림이 무엇인지, 그리고 시작하는 알파벳 문자를 말하세요.

❹ 대답이 옳으면 그 자리에 머물고, 틀렸거나 말하지 못하면 예전 위치로 돌아가세요.

❺ 먼저 도착하는 학생이 이기는 게임이에요.

Color the Leaves

준비물 : 색연필

❶ 각자 색연필을 준비하고 가위바위보를 한 후, 이긴 순서대로 원하는 번호를 부르세요.

❷ 자신이 부른 번호의 나뭇잎을 찾아 그림이 무엇인지, 그리고 시작하는 알파벳 문자를 말하세요.

❸ 대답이 옳으면 본인의 색연필로 나뭇잎을 색칠하고, 틀렸거나 말하지 못하면 다음 사람에게 기회를 넘기세요.

❹ 나뭇잎을 더 많이 색칠한 학생이 이기는 게임이에요.

Go Through the Wall

준비물 : 주사위, 마커

❶ 각자 마커를 정하고 가위바위보를 한 후, 이긴 순서대로 주사위를 굴리세요.

❷ 주사위의 수만큼 이동한 후 도착한 자리의 그림을 보고 그림이 무엇인지, 그리고 시작하는 알파벳 문자를 말하세요.

❸ 대답이 옳으면 그 자리에 머물고, 틀렸거나 말하지 못하면 예전 위치로 돌아가세요. 단, 화살표 꼬리가 있는 칸에 도착하면 화살표 머리쪽으로 올라갈 수 있고, 뱀의 꼬리가 있는 칸에 도착하면 뱀의 머리쪽으로 내려가야해요.

❹ 먼저 도착하는 학생이 이기는 게임이에요.

58

Let's Play a Card Game

준비물 : 가위

❶ 낱말 카드를 오려낸 후 책상 위에 그림이 보이도록 펼쳐 놓으세요.

❷ 선생님(혹은 진행자)이 그림 중 하나의 단어를 말하면 아는 학생은 알맞은 카드 위에 손을 올려 놓으세요.

❸ 손을 올려 놓은 학생은 다시 한 번 그 그림이 무엇인지, 그리고 시작하는 알파벳 문자를 말하세요.

❹ 대답이 옳으면 그 카드를 가질 수 있고, 틀렸거나 말하지 못하면 다음 사람에게 기회를 넘기세요.

❺ 더 많은 카드를 갖는 학생이 이기는 게임이에요.

Roller Coaster A1
Student Book

UNIT 01

PP. 12~13

A–a B–b C–c D–d E–e F–f

P. 14

🎧 apple / ant / arrow

P. 15

🎧 1. boy 2. ball 3. bee

P. 16

🎧 1. car 2. cook 3. bee 4. cap

1 ○ 2 X 3 X 4 ○

P. 17

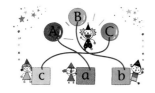

🎧 1. cook 2. arrow 3. ball 4. boy

1 ☑X 2 ☑X 3 ○☑ 4 ☑X

🎧 1. car 2. apple 3. ball

1 car, CAR 2 apple, APPLE 3 ball, BALL

P. 18

🎧 dog / dad / door

P. 19

🎧 1. egg 2. elephant 3. elbow

1 2 3

P. 20

🎧 1. fan 2. fish 3. flag

P. 21

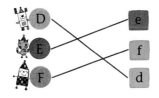

🎧 1. dad 2. fan 3. elbow 4. flag

1 ☑X 2 ☑X 3 ○☑ 4 ○☑

🎧 1. fish 2. elephant 3. door

1 fish, FISH 2 elephant, ELEPHANT
3 door, DOOR

UNIT 02

PP. 22~23

G–g   H–h   I–i   J–j   K–k   L–l

P. 24

1. goat   2. guitar   3. girl

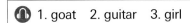

P. 25

hand / hat / house

P. 26

1. igloo   2. insect   3. iguana

2   3   1

P. 27

1. hand   2. girl   3. igloo   4. house

1 ☑ X   2 O ☒   3 O ☒   4 ☑ X

1. hat   2. goat   3. insect

1 <u>h</u>at, <u>H</u>AT   2 <u>g</u>oat, <u>G</u>OAT   3 <u>i</u>nsect, <u>I</u>NSECT

P. 28

1. jacket   2. juice   3. jeans   4. insect

1 O ☒   2 ☑ X   3 ☑ X   4 O ☒

P. 29

kitten / key / king

P. 30

1. lion   2. kitten   3. leaf   4. lily

1 O   2 X   3 X   4 O

P. 31

1. lily   2. juice   3. kitten   4. jacket

1 ☑ X   2 O ☒   3 ☑ X   4 O ☒

1. lion   2. key   3. jeans

1 <u>l</u>ion, <u>L</u>ION   2. <u>k</u>ey, <u>K</u>EY   3 <u>j</u>eans, <u>J</u>EANS

UNIT 03

PP. 32~33

M–m   N–n   O–o   P–p   Q–q   R–r   S–s

P. 34

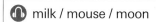 milk / mouse / moon

P. 35

🎧 1. nest   2. mouse   3. nurse   4. nose

1 ○   2 X   3 ○   4 X

P. 36

🎧 1. orange   2. ostrich   3. octopus

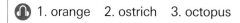

1   2   3

P. 37

🎧 1. milk   2. nest   3. nurse   4. moon

1 m̲ilk   2 n̲est   3 n̲urse   4 m̲oon

🎧 1. ostrich   2. nose   3. mouse

1 o̲strich, O̲STRICH
2 n̲ose, N̲OSE
3 m̲ouse, M̲OUSE

P. 38

🎧 1. pear   2. orange   3. pig   4. piano

1. O X̶   2. O X̶   3. ☑ X   4. ☑ X

P. 39

🎧 1. quilt   2. question   3. queen   4. pig

1 ○   2 ○   3 X   4 X

P. 40

🎧 robot / rose / rabbit

P. 41

🎧 1. socks   2. sun   3. shoes

PP. 42~43

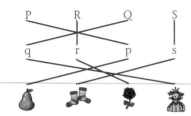

P   R   Q   S
q   r   p   s

🎧 1. pig   2. question   3. pear
   4. queen   5. quilt   6. piano

1 ☐O ☒X 2 ☑O ☐X 3 ☐O ☒X
4 ☑O ☐X 5 ☑O ☐X 6 ☑O ☐X

🎧 1. rabbit   2. sun   3. socks
   4. robot   5. rose   6. shoes

1 [r]abbit   2 [s]un
3 [s]ocks   4 [r]obot
5 [r]ose   6 [s]hoes

🎧 1. quilt   2. piano   3. robot
   4. rose   5. pear   6. shoes

1 <u>q</u>uilt, <u>Q</u>UILT
2 <u>p</u>iano, <u>P</u>IANO
3 <u>r</u>obot, <u>R</u>OBOT
4 <u>r</u>ose, <u>R</u>OSE
5 <u>p</u>ear, <u>P</u>EAR
6 <u>s</u>hoes, <u>S</u>HOES

UNIT 04

PP. 44~45

T–t U–u V–v W–w X–x Y–y Z–z

P. 46

🎧 tent / table / tiger

P. 47

🎧 1. ugly 2. table 3. umbrella 4. up

1 X   2 X   3 O   4 O

P. 48

🎧 1. vest 2. van 3. violin

P. 49

🎧 1. ugly 2. tiger 3. table 4. up

1 [u]gly   2 [t]iger
3 [t]able   4 [u]p

1. violin   2. tent   3. umbrella

1 violin, VIOLIN
2 tent, TENT
3 umbrella, UMBRELLA

P. 50

1. wolf   2. violin   3. witch   4. web

1 ☑X   2 O☒   3 O☒   4 ☑X

P. 51

1. ox   2. box   3. fox

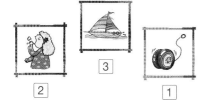

1   2   3

P. 52

1. yo-yo   2. yawn   3. yacht

3
2   1

P. 53

1. zoo   2. zipper   3. yacht   4. zebra

1 X   2 O   3 X   4 O

PP. 54~55

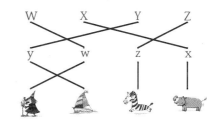

W   X   Y   Z
y   w   z   x

1. wolf   2. box   3. web
4. fox   5. ox   6. witch

1. ☑X   2. O☒   3. ☑X
4. O☒   5. ☑X   6. ☑X

1. yo-yo   2. zebra   3. yawn
4. zipper   5. zoo   6. yacht

1 [y]o-yo   2 [z]ebra
3 [y]awn   4 [z]ipper
5 [z]oo   6 [y]acht

1. witch   2. yo-yo   3. zipper
4. ox   5. yawn   6. web

1 witch, WITCH
2 yo-yo, YO-YO
3 zipper, ZIPPER
4 ox, OX
5 yawn, YAWN
6 web, WEB

Workbook

P. 1

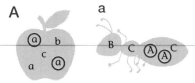

apple, <u>A</u>PPLE ant, <u>A</u>NT arrow, <u>A</u>RROW

P. 2

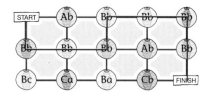

boy, <u>B</u>OY bee, <u>B</u>EE ball, <u>B</u>ALL

P. 3

cap, <u>C</u>AP car, <u>C</u>AR cook, <u>C</u>OOK

P. 6

dog, <u>D</u>OG dad, <u>D</u>AD door, <u>D</u>OOR

P. 7

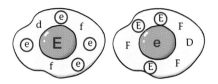

elbow, <u>E</u>LBOW egg, <u>E</u>GG elephant, <u>E</u>LEPHANT

P. 8

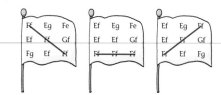

flag, <u>F</u>LAG fish, <u>F</u>ISH fan, <u>F</u>AN

UNIT 02

P. 11

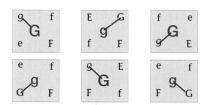

girl, <u>G</u>IRL goat, <u>G</u>OAT guitar, <u>G</u>UITAR

P. 12

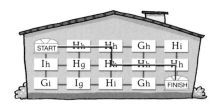

house, <u>H</u>OUSE hand, <u>H</u>AND hat, <u>H</u>AT

P. 13

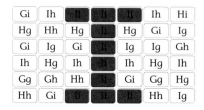

iguana, <u>I</u>GUANA insect, <u>I</u>NSECT
igloo, <u>I</u>GLOO

P. 16

jacket, <u>J</u>ACKET jeans, <u>J</u>EANS juice, <u>J</u>UICE

P. 17

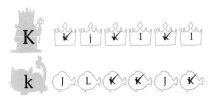

kitten, <u>K</u>ITTEN king, <u>K</u>ING key, <u>K</u>EY

P. 18

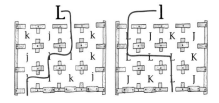

leaf, <u>L</u>EAF lily, <u>L</u>ILY lion, <u>L</u>ION

UNIT 03

P. 21

mouse, <u>M</u>OUSE milk, <u>M</u>ILK moon, <u>M</u>OON

P. 22

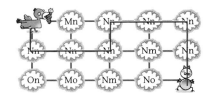

nest, <u>N</u>EST nose, <u>N</u>OSE nurse, <u>N</u>URSE

P. 23

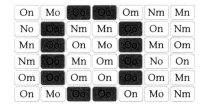

ostrich, <u>O</u>STRICH orange, <u>O</u>RANGE
octopus, <u>O</u>CTOPUS

P. 26

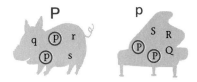

pig, <u>P</u>IG piano, <u>P</u>IANO pear, <u>P</u>EAR

P. 27

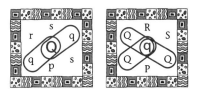

question, <u>Q</u>UESTION queen, <u>Q</u>UEEN
quilt, <u>Q</u>UILT

P. 28

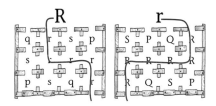

rabbit, <u>R</u>ABBIT robot, <u>R</u>OBOT rose, <u>R</u>OSE

P. 29

sun, <u>S</u>UN socks, <u>S</u>OCKS shoes, <u>SH</u>OES

P. 32

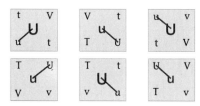

tiger, <u>T</u>IGER   table, <u>T</u>ABLE   tent, <u>T</u>ENT

P. 33

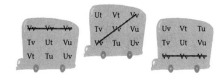

up, UP   umbrella, <u>U</u>MBRELLA   ugly, <u>U</u>GLY

P. 34

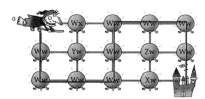

vest, <u>V</u>EST   violin, <u>V</u>IOLIN   van, <u>V</u>AN

P. 37

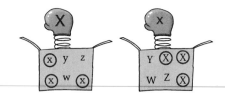

wolf, <u>W</u>OLF   witch, <u>W</u>ITCH   web, <u>W</u>EB

P. 38

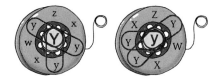

fo<u>x</u>, FO<u>X</u>   o<u>x</u>, O<u>X</u>   bo<u>x</u>, BO<u>X</u>

P. 39

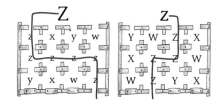

<u>y</u>awn, <u>Y</u>AWN   <u>y</u>o-yo, <u>Y</u>O-YO   <u>y</u>acht, <u>Y</u>ACHT

P. 40

zebra, ZEBRA   zipper, ZIPPER   zoo, ZOO

Achievement Test

1. d	2. I	3. h	4. g
5. ⓐ	6. ⓑ	7. ⓒ	8. ⓑ
9. ⓒ	10. ⓑ	11. ⓐ	12. ⓑ

Final Test

1. ⓑ	2. ⓒ	3. ⓒ	4. ⓐ
5. ⓑ	6. ⓐ	7. ⓒ	8. ⓐ
9. ⓑ	10. ⓒ	11. ⓐ	12. ⓑ

Final Test

Name

Score

[1-2] Choose the correct partner letter.

1. M [ ]

   ⓐ n   ⓑ m   ⓒ w

2. [ ] q

   ⓐ O   ⓑ P   ⓒ Q

[3-4] Choose the wrong partner letters.

3. ⓐ R – r   ⓑ X – x   ⓒ U – v

4. ⓐ S – z   ⓑ W – w   ⓒ K – k

[5-8] Choose the correct picture for the word.

5. wolf

   ⓐ    ⓑ    ⓒ

6. ostrich

   ⓐ   ⓑ    ⓒ

7. vest

ⓐ

ⓑ

ⓒ

8. dad

ⓐ

ⓑ

ⓒ

[9-12] **Choose the correct word for the picture.**

9.

ⓐ tiger   ⓑ zebra   ⓒ pig

10.

ⓐ cook   ⓑ queen   ⓒ nurse

11.

ⓐ umbrella   ⓑ violin   ⓒ tent

12.

ⓐ ox   ⓑ yacht   ⓒ insect

Achievement Test

Name

Score

[1–4] Check the correct partner letter.

1.

D

☐ b   ☐ d

2.

i

☐ L   ☐ I

3.

H

☐ h   ☐ k

4.

G

☐ a   ☐ g

[5–8] Choose the correct picture for the word.

5. key

ⓐ

ⓑ

ⓒ

6. cook

ⓐ

ⓑ

ⓒ

7. girl

ⓐ 　　ⓑ 　　ⓒ

8. lion

ⓐ 　　ⓑ 　　ⓒ

[9-12] Choose the correct word for the picture.

9.

ⓐ bee　　ⓑ dog　　ⓒ fish

10.

ⓐ fish　　ⓑ flag　　ⓒ lion

11.

ⓐ jacket　　ⓑ iguana　　ⓒ kitten

12.

ⓐ apple　　ⓑ ant　　ⓒ arrow

Stickers

A1

pp.12-13

a   b   c   d   e   f

pp.22-23

g   h   i   j   k   l

pp.32-33

m   n   o   p   q   r   s

pp.44-45

t   u   v   w   x   y   z

Roller Coaster

WORKBOOK

A Successful Start to Study English

Roller Coaster is a six-level series for elementary school students who are learning English as a foreign language. This series teaches all four languages skills: listening, speaking, reading, and writing. Students experience the language in a meaningful way through dialogs, songs, chants, games, and a variety of activities.

A1

01 Aa

Circle and Write

A

a b
c
a a

a

B C A A C

A

a

Write

___pple

___PPLE

2

___nt

___NT

3

___rrow

___RROW

Bb

Follow and Write

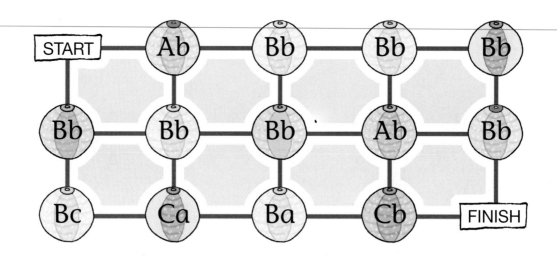

B

b

Write

1

___oy

___OY

2

___ee

___EE

3

___all

___ALL

Cc

Check and Write

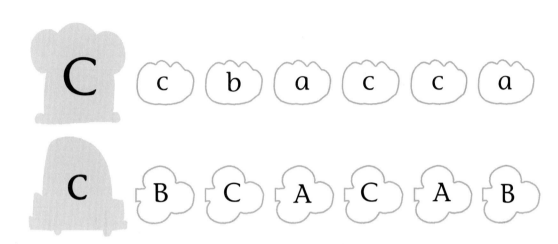

C c b a c c a

C B C A C A B

C

c

Write

1

___ap
___AP

2

___ar
___AR

3

___ook
___OOK

Aa | Bb | Cc

Trace and Write

1  apple

2  ant

3  arrow

4  boy

4

5   bee

6   ball

7   cap

8   car

9   cook

Dd

Join and Write

D
⌐⌐⌐⌐⌐

d

Write

1 _____og

_____OG

2 _____ad

_____AD

3 _____oor

_____OOR

Ee

Circle and Write

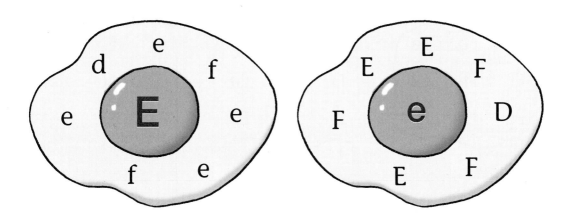

E

e

Write

1
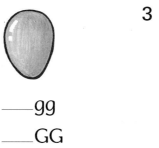
___lbow
___LBOW

2
___gg
___GG

3

___lephant
___LEPHANT

Ff

Draw a Line and Write

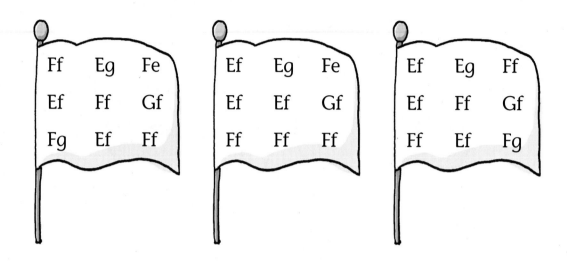

Ff	Eg	Fe
Ef	Ff	Gf
Fg	Ef	Ff

Ef	Eg	Fe
Ef	Ef	Gf
Ff	Ff	Ff

Ef	Eg	Ff
Ef	Ff	Gf
Ff	Ef	Fg

F

f

Write

1

___lag
___LAG

2

___ish
___ISH

3

___an
___AN

8

Dd | Ee | Ff

Trace and Write

1  dog

2  dad

3  door

4  elbow

5 egg

6  elephant

7 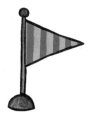 flag

8  fish

9 fan

02 Gg

Match and Write

g f **G** e F	E G **g** f F	f e **G** g E
e f **g** G F	g E **G** F f	e f **g** F G

G

g

Write

1

___irl

___IRL

2

___oat

___OAT

3

___uitar

___UITAR

Hh

Follow and Write

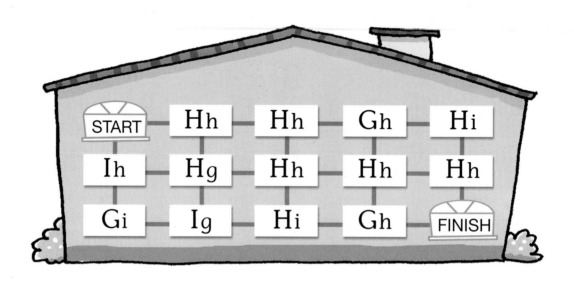

H

h

Write

1

____ouse
____OUSE

2

____and
____AND

3

____at
____AT

I i

Color and Write

Gi	Ih	Ii	Ii	Ii	Ih	Hi
Hg	Hh	Hg	Ii	Hg	Gi	Ig
Gi	Ig	Gi	Ii	Ig	Ig	Gh
Ih	Hg	Ih	Ii	Ih	Hg	Ih
Gg	Gh	Hh	Ii	Gi	Gg	Hg
Hh	Gi	Ii	Ii	Ii	Hh	Ig

I

i

Write

1

___guana
___GUANA

2

___nsect
___NSECT

3

___gloo
___GLOO

Gg Hh Ii

Trace and Write

1  girl

2  goat

3  guitar

4  house

5  hand

6  hat

7  iguana

8  insect

9  igloo

J j

Circle and Write

 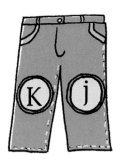  

J

j

Write

1

___acket

___ACKET

2

___eans

___EANS

3

___uice

___UICE

Kk

Check and Write

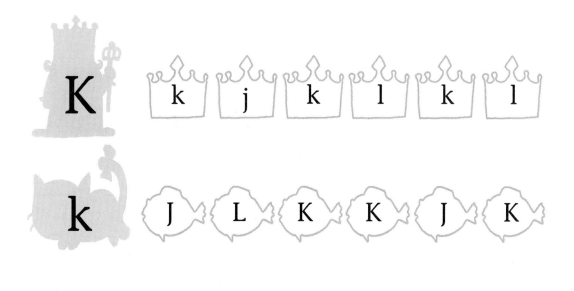

K

k

Write

1

___itten

___ITTEN

2
___ing

___ING

3

___ey

___EY

Ll

Follow and Write

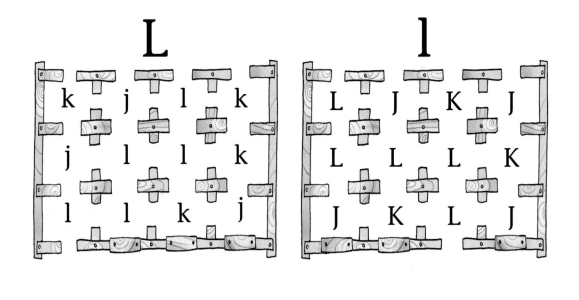

L
_____

l
_____

Write

1

___eaf

___EAF

2

___ily

___ILY

3

___ion

___ION

18

Jj Kk Ll

Trace and Write

1. jacket

2. jeans

3. juice

4. kitten

5  king _____

6  key _____

7  leaf _____

8  lily _____

9  lion _____

03 Mm

Draw a Line and Write

Mm	Mn	Nm
Mo	Mm	Om
No	On	Mm

Nm	Mn	Nm
Mo	On	Om
Mm	Mm	Mm

On	Mn	Nm
Mm	Mm	Mm
Nm	No	Mn

M

m

Write

1

____ouse
____OUSE

2

____ilk
____ILK

3

____oon
____OON

Nn

Follow and Write

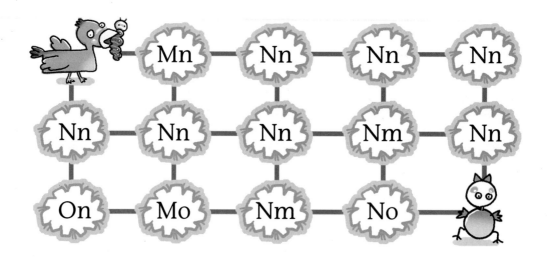

N

n

Write

1

_____est
_____EST

2

_____ose
_____OSE

3

_____urse
_____URSE

Oo

Color and Write

On	Mo	Oo	Oo	Om	Nm	Mn
No	Oo	Nm	Mn	Oo	On	Nm
Mn	Oo	On	Mo	Oo	Mn	Om
Nm	Oo	Mn	Om	Oo	No	On
Om	Oo	Om	On	Oo	Om	Mn
On	Mo	Oo	Oo	On	Mo	Nm

O

O

Write

1
___strich
___STRICH

2
___range
___RANGE

3
___ctopus
___CTOPUS

Mm | Nn | Oo

Trace and Write

1   mouse

2   milk

3   moon

4   nest

5   nose

6   nurse

7   ostrich

8   orange

9   octopus

Pp

Circle and Write

P

q p r
p s

p

S
P R
P Q

P

p

Write

1

___ig
___IG

2

___iano
___IANO

3

___ear
___EAR

Qq

Join and Write

Q

q

Write

1 ____uestion

____UESTION

2 ____ueen

____UEEN

3 ____uilt

____UILT

Rr

Follow and Write

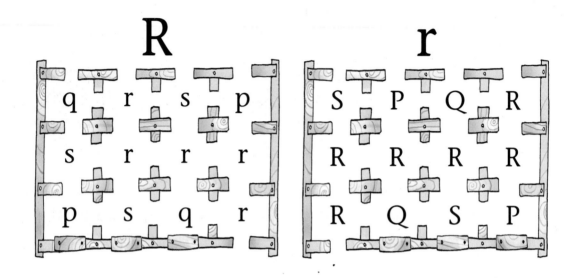

R

r

Write

1 ___abbit
___ABBIT

2 ___obot
___OBOT

3 ___ose
___OSE

Ss

Circle and Write

S

s

Write

1	2	3

___un	___ocks	___hoes
___UN	___OCKS	___HOES

Pp | Qq | Rr | Ss

Trace and Write

1   pig

2   piano

3   pear

4   question

5   queen

6   quilt

7 rabbit

8 robot

9 rose

10 sun

11 socks

12 shoes

Color and Write

Vt	Tu	Tt	Tt	Tt	Vt	Tv
Uv	Vt	Uv	Tt	Uv	Tu	Vt
Uu	Ut	Tu	Tt	Ut	Uv	Vu
Ut	Vu	Uv	Tt	Tu	Ut	Tu
Vu	Tv	Ut	Tt	Tu	Uv	Vt
Uv	Uv	Vt	Tt	Vt	Ut	Uv

T

t

Write

1

___iger
___IGER

2

___able
___ABLE

3

___ent
___ENT

Uu

Match and Write

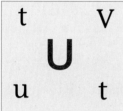 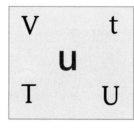 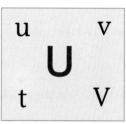

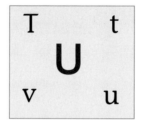 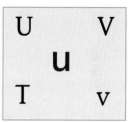

U

u

Write

1

___p
___P

2

___mbrella
___MBRELLA

3

___gly
___GLY

V v

Draw a Line and Write

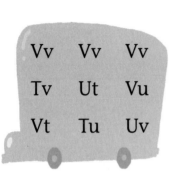

Vv	Vv	Vv
Tv	Ut	Vu
Vt	Tu	Uv

Ut	Vt	Vv
Tv	Vv	Vu
Vv	Tu	Uv

Uv	Vt	Tu
Tv	Ut	Vu
Vv	Vv	Vv

V

v

Write

1

____est

____EST

2

____iolin

____IOLIN

3

____an

____AN

Tt | Uu | Vv

Trace and Write

1

tiger

2

table

3

tent

4

up

5  umbrella

6 ugly

7  vest

8  violin

9  van

W w

Follow and Write

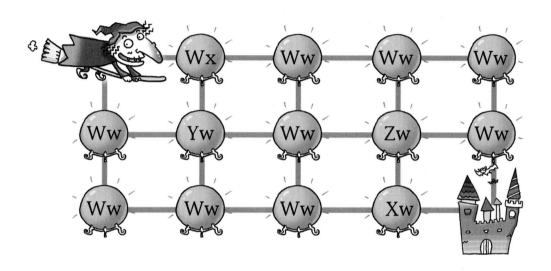

W

w

Write

1

____olf

____OLF

2

____itch

____ITCH

3

____eb

____EB

X x

Circle and Write

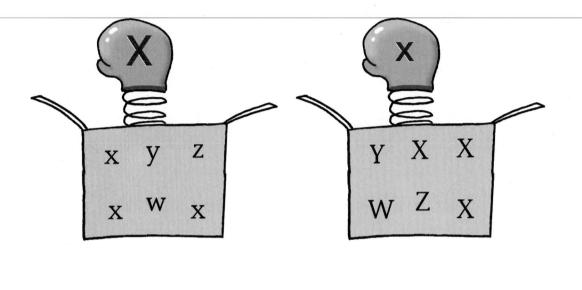

X

x

Write

1   fo___
     FO___

2   o___
     O___

3   bo___
     BO___

Y y

Join and Write

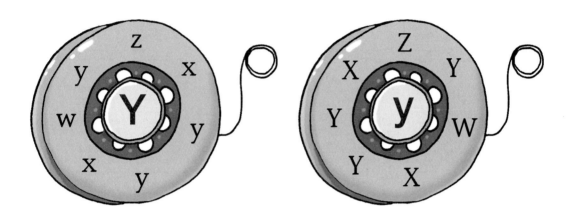

Y

y

Write

1

___awn

___AWN

2

___o-yo

___O-YO

3

___acht

___ACHT

Zz

Follow and Write

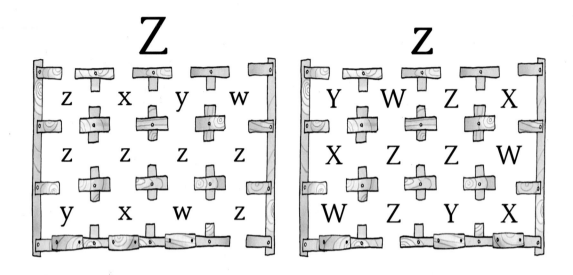

Z

Z

Write

1 _____ebra
_____EBRA

2 _____ipper
_____IPPER

3 _____oo
_____OO

Ww Xx Yy Zz

Trace and Write

1. wolf

2. witch

3. web

4. fox

5. ox

6. box

7 yawn

8 yo-yo

9 yacht

10 zebra

11 zipper

12 zoo

Write Aa to Zz

Roller Coaster

A Successful Start to Study English